Here's Your Sign!™

Here's Your Sign!™

Bill Engvall

Illustrations by
Bill Ross

RUTLEDGE HILL PRESS
Nashville, Tennessee
A Division of Thomas Nelson Publishers
Since 1798

www.thomasnelson.com

Published by Rutledge Hill Press, a Division of Thomas Nelson, Inc., P.O. Box 141000, Nashville, Tennessee 37214.

Rutledge Hill Press books may be purchased in bulk for educational, business, fundraising, or sales promotional use. For information, please e-mail SpecialMarkets@ThomasNelson.com.

Library of Congress Cataloging-in-Publication Data

Engvall, Bill.
    Here's your sign! / Bill Engvall ; illustrations by Bill Ross.
      p. cm.
    ISBN 1-4016-0234-7 (pbk.)
    1. Stupidity—Humor.   I. Ross, Bill, 1956–   . II. Title.
PN6231.S77E54 2005
818'.602—dc22   2005017088

Printed in the United States of America
05 06 07 08 09 — 5 4 3 2

This book is dedicated to all those who love to laugh. Thanks for allowing me to do the thing that I love the most—making you laugh. Enjoy!

WARNING!

Use of this product may cause shortness of breath or milk to spurt out your nose. In extreme cases, a busted gut may result. Discontinue use and consult your mom immediately!

Introduction

Stupid people are much more clever than most folks give them credit for. As masters of disguise, they blend in naturally with almost any crowd. They can carry on intelligent conversations, drive flashy cars, and wear expensive clothes. Some even have college degrees and professional jobs. But don't be fooled—it's only a scam.

Stupid people wait around, hiding, fading into their surroundings, hoping someone will mistake them for a normal person. Then, when they run into a *real* normal person, the stupid person pounces like a pig on a peanut with a dumb question that you just can't believe.

One day last summer, for instance, I got a flat tire. Fortunately, I was close to a gas station and so I just pulled the car into the lot. An attendant walked out, looked at the tire, and—I swear—he asked me, "Tire go flat?" I kept as straight a face as I could and replied, "No, I was just driving down the road when all of a sudden those other three just swelled right up on me." I figured that would leave him stumped. But he never even batted an eyelash. He just nodded his head and said, "Yep. The heat'll do that." What else could I say? I just reached into my briefcase and handed him his very own Stupid sign.

You see, to protect us ordinary, normal folks, stupid people ought to have to wear signs that say, "I'm stupid." That way they couldn't sneak up on us and we would never, ever have to depend on them for anything. We could see them coming. If you wanted to ask directions, for instance, you could say, "Oh, wait a minute—I didn't see your sign. Never mind. I'll ask someone else."

To make the world a safer place to live, I'm here to give out Stupid signs. Let me tell you about some of the very stupid people I've met.

We were having a small earthquake the other day and my wife asked, "Is this an earthquake?" I said, "Nope. I just put a quarter in the vibrating house machine."

As I was lying on the beach in Hawaii, I heard a man a couple of yards away say to his wife, "You know, for all the tourists here, you don't see a lot of out-of-state license plates." I didn't have to say anything. I just handed him a Stupid sign.

My wife and I had just parked our car and were walking into a hotel for a New Year's Eve party when the doorman asked, "Are you going to celebrate the new year?" I said, "No, we're going to attend a wake for the old year."

When my wife was expecting our first child, a woman walked up to her and asked, "Oh, are you pregnant?" My wife said, "No, I'm practicing to smuggle basketballs into Cuba."

I took my family on a trip in an RV to Las Vegas, where it was 120 degrees. The guard at the RV park asked, "Will you be using your air conditioner?" I said, "No, ma'am, we just drove in from the face of the sun and we're trying to acclimate ourselves."

My wife and I were shopping in a department store and I had three pairs of pants on my arm. The salesperson asked, "Do you want to try those on?" I said, "No, I'm just trying to keep my arm warm."

I was taking a deer to the taxidermist when a lady looked in the back of my truck and asked, "Did you shoot that deer?" I said, "Nope. He hopped in the back of the truck, handed me a note, and killed himself."

I drove out to the lake near where we live and was walking down the dock holding a fishing pole. A guy asked me, "Are you going fishing? "I said, "Nope. I'm taking the worms waterskiing."

I was at a parachuting school the other day walking around with a parachute on my back. A guy asked me, "Are you going to jump out of a plane?" I said, "No, I wear this when I walk because it helps me to slow down."

Last winter my kids and I were making a snowman in the front yard. A woman walked by and asked, "Are you going to build a snowman?" I said, "No, we're just rolling snow off the yard."

When I was at the vet's the other day, I overheard the doctor tell a woman, "Give your dog one pill twice a day." She looked puzzled and asked, "How do I give her the same pill twice?"

I was sitting in the exit row on a plane to Seattle. The man across the aisle recognized me and asked, "Are you going to Seattle?" I said, "Nope. I'm going to San Francisco. I'll be parachuting out in about an hour."

"Dad, What Is Sex?"

When my daughter was at the age where she was just starting to figure stuff out—about eight or nine—she was usually polite enough to leave us out of her wonderings. But occasionally, she came and asked a question.

One day, just after breakfast, she came into the kitchen and asked, "Dad, what is sex?"

After I spit coffee all over the counter, I had to peel my wife off the ceiling. She kept saying, "I told you she saw us! I told you so!"

While our little girl was looking at her mother trying to figure out why she was so upset, I lovingly put my hand on her head and asked, "Where did you hear about this?"

She said, "Daddy, my friend at school said that sex is when a man and a woman kiss and then wrestle around."

I figure it all depends on how well you wrestle, but that definition was as good as any I'd heard from a nine-year-old. And I told her so.

My wife took off her swimsuit after we had spent a day at the beach and I said, "Wow, you sure got sunburned!" She answered, "Wrong! I didn't get sunburned. I just got my butt bleached."

I was on my way to play tennis the other day and a guy asked me, "Is that your tennis racquet?" I said, "No, it's a can't-miss flyswatter."

When I was flying to Hawaii, we hit some turbulence at 35,000 feet. The man next to me looked out his window. "What was that?" he asked, clearly worried. I said, "Oh my goodness, we just hit a dog!"

I was spraying an insecticide on the flowers in our backyard and my neighbor asked, "Are you killing bugs?" I said, "No, I'm just trying to get them drunk and hope they drive home."

The other day my wife and I were watching TV and she said, "You know, you never see the pope with his wife." I said, "That's because she stays at home putting sequins on his hats and robes. Besides, she has to take care of his kids."

The other day I was cutting the grass in the front yard when a friend dropped by and asked, "Mowing the yard?" "No," I said. "I'm just running oil through the lawn mower."

The other day my friend and I were standing on the street corner when the cops dragged this guy out of a store in a headlock and handcuffs. My friend asked, "Do you think they are taking him to jail?" "No," I said. "He's an escape artist and they want to see how long it takes him to get free."

Have you ever had someone call your house and when you answer the phone they ask, "Are you home?" Just say, "Nope. I'm on Mars and had my calls forwarded."

Last year when my wife and I were going home for Thanksgiving, a man pulled up next to us at a stoplight with a dead deer on the hood of his car. My wife looked at me. "Do you think he's been hunting?" "No," I said. "They give away a deer with the purchase of every Jeep."

I cut my finger really badly the other day and went to the emergency room with a rag wrapped around my hand. The nurse looked at it and asked, "Did you cut yourself?" "Nope," I said. "I'm here to donate blood and I hate needles."

The other day we were setting up tables in our yard and putting out old furniture labeled with prices. My neighbor came over and asked, "Hey, are you having a yard sale?" I said, "No, we thought we would furnish the front yard and try renting it out for a while."

I was in the park flying a kite with my son. A guy walked up to us and asked, "Y'all flying a kite?" I said, "No, we're fishing for birds."

Parenting

When you are a parent, you need to be able to expertly handle situations you could never plan for. One night, for example, my two kids were taking a bath when I heard this bloodcurdling scream. It looked like someone had shot my daughter out of the tub from a cannon. Before I could even ask her what the problem was, I saw the problem floating in the bathwater. And while my daughter was screaming and running around like someone had just thrown sulfuric acid on her, my son, proud of his accomplishment, wanted to stay in the tub and play with his turd.

"Look, Daddy! Big boat!" he giggled as it floated around.

When I tried to get him out of the tub, he got all upset because he didn't understand why he couldn't stay in there and play with the "boat." Finally, after much calm and rational discussion, I got him out of the tub. It was then I faced one of those interesting parenting dilemmas that no one ever tells you about. I had to figure out whether to drain the tube first or capture the "treasure" as it floated around in the bathwater.

If this ever happens to you, the answer is to drain the tub first. I know. I've tried it both ways.

I thought I could walk three blocks to my friend's house without any problems, but halfway there the heavens opened up. So I was soaking wet when I walked in his front door. He looked at me and asked, "Is it raining?" "No," I answered. "I thought I would take the fish for a walk."

I was in the Atlanta airport and walked by the room reserved for smokers, which was literally filled with a cloud of smoke. A guy asked me, "Hey, is that the smoking room?" I said, "Nope. It's the fog simulation room."

I took my son to get a haircut and the barber asked, "Are you here for a haircut?" I said, "No, we just came here so that I could show my boy the blue water you keep the combs in."

I purchased a car, drove it home, and parked it in front of the house for all the world to see. My neighbor asked, "Hey, did you get a new car?" "No," I said. "I bought four new tires and the car came with them."

I was sitting in the living room watching the news the other day when my friend came in the front door and asked, "Are you watching TV?" "Nope," I said. "I'm watching the wall and the TV is in the way."

Last weekend I took my son camping and we had all the latest camping gear with us. We were unpacking our stuff when the park ranger walked up and asked, "Are you going camping?" I said, "No, I'm trying to open my own outdoors shop."

One night I was taking my dog for a walk around the block when my neighbor hollered at me, "Are you walking your dog?" I said, "No, I was walking the leash and the dog ran through it."

When I was in college, I got really drunk one night and woke up the next morning in front of the toilet. My roommate asked, "Are you sick?" I said, "No, I just wanted to see what the dog liked about this water."

Last December I came home from Christmas shopping with three bags of presents. My wife took one look at me and asked, "Did you buy anything?" I said, "Nope. I stole all this stuff and had it gift wrapped."

A guy walked off a plane with a lei around his neck. A lady waiting in line to get on the plane asked, "Have you guys been to Hawaii?" "No," he said. "We just flew through a garden."

I was at the zoo with my family and a woman asked me, "Is that a baby monkey?" I said, "No, we just haven't shaved our son yet."

I left my house dressed in camouflage and carrying a gun. My neighbor asked, "Are you going hunting?" I said, "No, I'm running late for my local militia meeting."

I went to the doctor's office last week. I walked up to the desk and the nurse asked, "Are you sick?" I said, "No, ma'am, I'm fine. I just came because I'm trying to catch something."

Not long ago I took my wife to a movie. While we were standing in line, the guy behind us asked, "Is this the line for movie tickets?" I said, "Nope. We're in line for the soup kitchen."

I walked into a barbershop and the barber asked, "Are you here to get a haircut?" I said, "No, my hair has been bad and I want you to threaten it."

I was looking through the humidor at the grocery store, picking out a couple of cigars, and a guy asked me, "Are you going to smoke those cigars?" I said, "No, I am going to plant them and see if more grow."

Reading

I never thought I would cuss Dr. Seuss, but after you've read *The Cat in the Hat* 40 times, it's inevitable. When you see your kid race into the room with that book under his arm, you think up some brand-new expletives to describe Dr. Seuss's ancestors. Nowadays, I see a kids' book and 15 minutes later I've got a beer in one hand and a cigarette in the other.

The problem is you can't just read the book to your child. You have to let your kid read it. Pretty soon, I'm like a Dallas Cowboys cheerleader. And it's not because I like to wear white boots and short shorts. I start coaxing him along, hoping he'll make that long-yardage play where he accidentally skips a few pages.

"You can do it!" I cheer as he struggles with a word or phrase.

But as the hours drag on, it turns into: "No, it's 'Go, dog, go! Go, dog, go!' for crying out loud. You just said it two pages ago! Memory, son, memory!"

I can't wait until he starts school so I can let his teachers take over where I left off. Hopefully, they can undo the damage I've done before it becomes a permanent learning disability.

The other night my wife was in the tub and I yelled through the bathroom door, "Are you taking a bath?" She said, "No, I'm scuba diving for sunken ships."

I went into my son's room and he was sitting at his desk with his textbook open, taking notes. I asked, "Are you doing homework?" He said, "No, I'm rewriting the end of my history book."

One night I walked into a bar and the bartender asked, "Can I get you something to drink?" I said, "Nope. Here's five bucks. I just want to watch other people drink."

I hadn't shaved for a couple of weeks and ran into a guy from my bowling team. He asked, "Are you growing a beard?" I said, "No, I'm growing sod for the front yard."

Several years ago I was in the mall pushing my baby son in a stroller when a lady stopped me and asked, "Do you know that your baby has your eyes?" "Well, that explains why I can't see," I said.

I was driving through New Jersey and pulled my car into a gas station. The attendant walked up and asked, "Fill it up?" I said, "No, just give me enough gas to make it halfway to the motel and I'll walk the rest of the way."

My wife and I were seated in a restaurant and the waiter came to our table and asked, "Would you like to order?" I said, "Nope. We just come into restaurants and check out the menu for typos."

A fire truck went flying past me with its siren going. My wife asked, "Do you think they're on the way to a fire?" I said, "No, they're just in a really fast parade."

I was watering the yard the other day and a kid asked, "Hey, Mister, are you watering the grass?" I said, "No, I'm flushing out the hose."

One winter it was really cold and we were driving through a hail storm. My wife asked, "Is that hail?" I said, "No, those are very little Ping-Pong balls."

I went to the doctor's office and the nurse asked, "Are you here to see the doctor?" I said, "No, I'm here to join the all-nurse choir."

I was in *my* backyard the other night looking through *my* telescope. My neighbor had just taken out his trash and came over and asked, "Are you looking at the stars?" I said, "No, I'm having a staring contest with a guy on Mars."

When my wife was expecting our first child she ran into a friend
of hers in a mall. The friend said, "I didn't know you were
pregnant." My wife said, "I'm not. It's just gas."

I was signing a credit card slip the other day when my pen stopped writing. So I started shaking the pen up and down. A lady asked, "Did your pen run out of ink?" I said, "No, my hand randomly starts doing the Macarena."

I was on a crowded plane and as the flight attendant pushed the meal cart down the aisle, the guy next to me asked, "Do you think that's got our food on it?" I said, "No, it's filled with circus clowns. They're going to do a show for us."

My wife and I were tilling the garden and our neighbor asked, "Are you going to plant something?" I said, "No, we're looking for moles."

I was putting on my Rollerblades the other day and a guy asked, "Hey, are you going inline skating?" I said, "No, I'm going dancing. These skates make it more of a challenge."

One night it snowed and the next day the kids and I went outside to make a snowman. After we finished, a guy walked by and asked, "Hey, did y'all build that snowman?" I said, "No, the flakes just randomly landed in this shape."

I was putting my luggage in the overhead bin on a plane when the flight attendant asked me, "Do you have a seat?" I looked at her and said, "No, I bought a standing-room-only ticket."

I went to the pet store to buy a chew toy for my dog. The clerk asked, "Is this for your dog?" I said, "Nope. It's for me. I am trying to quit chewing on the couch."

One day I was in the kitchen putting together a ham and cheese sandwich and my wife asked, "Are you making a sandwich?" I said, "No, I'm playing hide-and-seek with the ham."

I was making some dye for our Easter eggs and my wife asked, "Are you going to color those eggs?" I said, "No, we're going to leave them white and hide them in the snow."

I was driving one night in a really heavy rain. My car slid off the road into a field of tall grass. When the sheriff arrived he asked, "Slip off the road?" I said, "Nope. The car got hungry so I let it graze in the grass for a while."

Privacy

I've noticed that when you are a parent you can kiss your privacy good-bye. I fully understand now why my father used to lock the bathroom door. He wasn't embarrassed about anything—it was the only time he ever got to be alone.

I remember one morning I was taking a shower. I had the bathroom door shut, but somehow I had forgotten to lock it. All of a sudden, the shower curtain was ripped back and there stood my daughter with her friend!

Next thing I knew, the girls were marching back out the door and my daughter huffed, "See? I told you."

I never found out what that was all about, but I'll tell you something I did learn that day: there is absolutely no way for a wet, naked man to climb a tile wall. It just cannot be done.

I was in the bathroom and *my* son yelled through
the door, "Dad, are you going to the bathroom?" I said,
"Nope. I'm quilting the Charmin."

I drove through a drive-up window at a fast-food restaurant and the kid in the window asked, "Would you like to order?" I said, "No, I'm on a diet and thought I would just sit here awhile and think about french fries."

Several years ago I was standing in a phone booth looking in my wallet for a phone number. A lady walked up and asked, "Are you using the pay phone?" I said, "No, I'm standing here trying to turn into Superman."

I was waiting to get my hair cut the other day and a man asked, "Is that your real hair?" I said, "No, I'm the very first Chia person."

My wife and I were walking in our neighborhood with our dog
and a woman walked by and asked, "Are you walking your
dog?" I said, "No, we're out looking for Amelia Earhart."

I was putting my golf clubs in the car and my neighbor asked, "Are you going to play some golf?" I said, "Nope. I'm the caddy for the Invisible Man."

My daughter and I left the house carrying our ice skates. A lady walking by asked, "Are you going ice-skating?" I said, "No, we're going swimming the hard way."

My car broke down on the highway one day. I got out, opened the hood, and began looking for the problem. A guy stopped and asked, "Are you having car trouble?" I said, "No, I'm just showing off my engine."

I was in the backyard running one of those gas-powered log splitters that make a racket. My neighbor asked, "Hey, are you chopping wood?" I said, "Nope. I'm looking for termites."

I was on my knees in front of the fireplace with a bellows, trying to get a fire started, when my wife asked, "Are you building a fire?" I said, "No, I'm torturing the wood."

I was leaning over a water fountain when a guy behind me asked, "Are you getting a drink?" I said, "No, I'm trying to see the sewer through this little hole."

I was in my high school band and we had to wear one of those big fuzzy hats. I had one on and I remember a guy asking me, "Are you in the band?" I said, "No, I'm the youngest Shriner in town."

A lady was setting up an easel in the park. A guy walked up and asked, "Are you going to paint a picture?" She said, "No, I'm waiting for the art fairy to come by and do it."

I picked up my guitar and a guy asked if I was going to play it. I said, "Nope. I'm trying to scrape off my fingerprints."

I was wearing a Band-Aid and a guy at work asked, "Did you cut yourself?" I said, "No, I just like the feeling of my arm hair being ripped out when I take this off."

The other day I was sitting on the sofa watching the football game. My wife walked in and asked, "Are you watching TV?" I said, "No, I am trying to move it across the room with mental telepathy."

Goofy Warning Labels

I find it amazing that nearly every product we buy today is imprinted with those little "Warning" labels. You know what I'm talking about—labels such as, "Discharging this shotgun into your face could be harmful or fatal." It's obvious that most of us would know that. But for every silly product warning, you know that somewhere, some incredibly stupid person wrote the company a letter that began something like this: "I pointed your shotgun at my face and . . ."

Here are some of my favorites.

- On every tube of Preparation-H is a warning that says, "Do not take this product orally." Man, that's really sad! Can you imagine the letter that someone wrote the company? "I ate this whole tube of your product and I still have those darned hemorrhoids. And man, my mouth is so small that I can't even eat a jellybean. But I can whistle real good."

- On some blow-dryers is a warning not to use the dryer while you are in the shower. They're kidding, right? I mean, can you imagine standing in the shower after you have just finished shampooing your hair and yelling, "Hey, Honey! Toss me that blow-dryer, would you?"

  On other blow-dryers is a warning label that says, "Do not use this product while sleeping." Now that has become a real problem with

me! I can't tell you how many times I've awakened to find myself doing my hair—"Dang it! I was sleep-styling again!"

- On plastic bags you get from the dry cleaners is a warning label that says, "This bag is not a toy." Where the heck did that come from? Did they do a survey at a mall during Christmas? I can just see some youngster perched on Santa's lap saying, "No, Santa, I don't want a bike or a train. Just get me a big old clear dry cleaning bag!"

- On cans of shaving cream I've seen warning labels that say, "Avoid spraying this near an open flame." Where was the guy who wrote that letter shaving? He must have been sitting around the campfire one night when he got to feeling a little bristly. "Hey, Bubba, toss me that can of shaving cream! I believe I'm going to freshen up before we turn in."

- On the back of a car fan-belt package I read a warning sign once that actually said, "Stop motor before applying this product." Wouldn't you love to have been there the first time *that* happened? Some guy walks into the garage office, his hands are all cut up and bloody. The boss says, "Walt! What happened, man?" Walt looks up sheepishly as he applies a tourniquet to his arm and says, "Look here, boys. Let me give y'all a little tip. If you're gonna put a fan belt on a car, you'd better shut the motor off first! You can't stop it with your hands, man. It's like a machine or something."

- In a lot of boxes with electronic equipment—or even shoes—are little packets of a drying agent. And right there, for everyone to see, is a warning label that says, "Do not eat this!" How many times have you ever bought a pair of shoes thinking that there just might be something to eat in there? But some lady somewhere opened up a shoebox once and said, "Oh, look here! I got a new pair of pumps *and* a pack of Chiclets!"

My family was getting packed up while I was putting our skis on the top rack of the car. My neighbor saw me and asked, "Hey, are you guys going skiing?" I said, "Nope. I put these on top of the car in case it flips over on the snow."

I was taking my son to hockey practice the other day and a guy asked, "Hey, is that your hockey stick?" My son said, "No, it's a really big boomerang."

I was setting out a mousetrap in the kitchen and my son asked if I was trying to catch a mouse. I said, "No, I'm setting up an obstacle course for when I get up in the dark."

My wife was at the manicurist and put her hands on the table. A woman asked her, "Are you getting your nails done?" My wife said, "No, I'm here to have the backs of my hands read."

I was in the bathroom lathering up my face the other day and my son asked, "Dad, are you shaving?" I said, "No, son, I'm just putting on a really cheap Santa Claus disguise."

When I was in college, I took some clothes home to my mother's house to be washed. She asked if they were dirty. I said, "Nope. They're clean. I just like to wear them really wrinkled."

My wife and I went out the other night. We saw this car with six kids in it and they had pulled up onto one of those parking curbs. My wife asked, "Is your car stuck?" One kid replied, "No, it's a new teeter-totter from Ford."

I was in Sears and put some things on the checkout counter.
The clerk asked, "Are you going to buy those?" I said, "No, I'm
going to steal them, but I just wanted you to see them first."

I had my dog all soaped up in the bathtub the other night. My daughter looked in and asked, "Are you washing the dog?" I said, "No, I thought I would lather him up and put him in the front yard as a snow dog."

My family was camping and I was arranging the wood so that I could light a fire. My wife asked, "Are you going to build a fire?" I said, "No, I'm making a tepee for ants."

My son, whose front tooth had just come out, was with me in a mall. I ran in to a friend of mine who looked at my son and asked, "Did you lose your tooth?" My son said, "No, I like to keep that space open so I can spit water through it."

One summer I was walking out to the pool at the hotel where we were staying, dressed in my swimsuit. A guy sitting in a lounge chair asked, "Going swimming?" I said, "No, I'm just a really shy streaker."

White Trash Barbie

To tell you the truth, I really hate Barbie dolls. They're just too fluffy and frilly for my taste. I think they ought to come out with a more realistic Barbie doll. Why isn't there a "White Trash Barbie"?

This is Barbie in her later years. The modeling career is over, and Barbie and Ken live in a Barbie double-wide. They could call it the "Dream Trailer." That Corvette would be on blocks in the front yard with the fenders mashed in and the back window shot out.

Of course, Ken would have a big old beer belly, wear dirty white T-shirts, and spend a lot of time scratching himself and belching.

"What's for supper tonight, Barbie?"

Barbie'd stick her head out the screen door, hair in curlers, and say, "Fish sticks."

Ken would probably grin and say, "Fish sticks? What? Is it our anniversary again?"

And imagine all the accessories you'd have to go along with White Trash Barbie. You could have a little police car that would pull up in front of the mobile home from time to time because Ken got drunk and started yelling at Barbie.

Then, the cops could lead Ken off in some little Ken-cuffs. Meanwhile, Ken would still be yelling at Barbie, "I know you slept with G.I. Joe! I know you did!"

And Barbie would be crying, sitting on the wooden steps, "Oh, don't take him away. I love him. He didn't mean it, I know he didn't."

My friend was over at the house yesterday and our cat walked into the room. My friend asked, "Is that your cat?" I said, "No, it's a rat that just climbed out of the dryer."

I went to church on crutches last Sunday. The usher asked me, "Did you hurt your leg?" I said, "No, I just like the chafing under my arms."

I was running through the airport when a guy asked me, "Are you late for your plane?" I said, "No, they're having a sale at the duty-free shop and I want to get there before all the good stuff is gone."

I was sitting in *my* easy chair with a book the other day when a friend walked in the front door and asked, "Are you reading that book?" I said, "Nope. I'm waiting for a fly to land in it so I can squish him."

I was carrying out a bag of garbage the other day and my
neighbor yelled across the fence, "Are you taking out the
trash?" I said, "No, I'm going to feed our pet rats."

A guy was walking around with one of those cheese hats on and somebody said, "Hey, are you a Packers fan?" He said, "No, I just like the body that cheese gives my hair."

The last time I took my dog to the vet's office a woman in the waiting room asked, "Is your dog sick?" I said, "No, he just likes to come here to visit the other dogs."

My cat was on the porch meowing at the front door and my wife asked, "Is the cat outside?" I said, "No, that's the new doorbell I just put in."

I was taking my son to the baseball game the other day and he had his glove on. My neighbor saw us and asked, "Are you going to the game?" I said, "No, he likes to have his glove in the car with him in case someone throws a ball at us."

I was wearing some new tennis shoes and my friend asked, "Did you get new shoes?" I said, "No, I just stepped in a puddle of Liquid Paper."

I was taking the collection bag off the lawn mower last summer and my neighbor asked, "Did you just mow the yard?" I said, "Nope. I'm spreading these grass clippings on the ground to see if they will grow."

One time when I was on the platform at the train station, a guy came up to me and asked, "Are you going to catch the train?" I said, "No, I'm going to wait for it to start moving and then race it."

I was making breakfast the other day and was cracking some eggs. My daughter walked into the kitchen and asked, "Are you going to fry those eggs?" I said, "No, I'm looking for baby chicks."

I walked into the bedroom the other morning with a toothbrush in one hand and a tube of toothpaste in the other. My wife asked, "Are you going to brush your teeth?" I said, "No, I'm going to make a toothpaste sculpture."

My car was parked in the driveway with the hood up. My neighbor walked by and asked, "Are you working on your car?" I said, "No, it's just more of a challenge to drive it this way."

I was talking on the phone last night when my wife came in and asked, "Are you on the phone?" I said, "No, I superglued the receiver to my ear so I won't have to pick it up the next time."

I took a friend of mine waterskiing. While he was in the water putting his skis on, another boat came by and the driver yelled, "Hey! Y'all going to water-ski?" I said, "Nope. We're trolling for alligators and my friend's the bait."

When my son was younger, I took him out one Halloween. The third house we stopped at, the lady came to the door and asked, "Are you trick-or-treating?" I said, "No, he's in the witness protection program."

My daughter and I were in the backyard stargazing when my wife asked, "Are you looking at the stars?" I said, "No, we're trying to look over the top of our own heads."

The big tree in my front yard was dying and I was taking it down myself with a new chain saw. There were sections of tree lying everywhere when my neighbor asked, "Are you cutting down that tree?" I said, "No, I'm putting one up."

We had our house painted green while my neighbor was on vacation. When he came back he asked why our house was green. I said, "Because it's sick."

I was sitting in the waiting room at the bus station and a guy asked me, "Are you waiting for the bus?" I said, "No, I'm auditioning for the next *Speed* movie."

My wife and I were driving to the store and I turned on the left-hand-turn signal. My wife asked, "Are you going to turn left?" I said, "Nope. I just like to see if the signal is keeping time with the song on the radio."

I was digging dandelions out of my front yard and my neighbor walked over and asked, "Are you pulling weeds?" I said, "No, I'm sending them to a weed relocation center."

I was standing on a chair unscrewing a lightbulb when my wife asked if I was changing the bulb. I said, "No, I thought I'd stick my finger in the socket and give myself an Afro."

I was in the front yard with a basket of Easter eggs getting ready for our annual Easter egg hunt. My neighbor asked, "Are you going to hide those eggs?" I said, "No, we're going to leave the eggs out and hide the baskets."

When the Super Bowl was played in Jacksonville, I was able to get some tickets and showed them to a friend. He asked, "Are those Super Bowl tickets?" I said, "No, they're tickets to the couch in my den."

I was walking into a cafeteria and a lady asked, "Are you going to get something to eat?" I said, "No, I just like the thrill of standing in line to look at food."

I was cleaning my deer rifle and my friend asked, "Is that your gun?" I said, "No, it's a bow and arrow disguised as a rifle."

We had a really bad storm the other night. At one point there was a bright flash of light and my son asked, "Was that lightning?" I said, "No, the sun just blew out."

I was lying in bed one morning thinking about getting up and my wife asked, "Are you going to just lie in that bed all day?" I said, "Nope. I'm having an out-of-body experience and my soul is actually at work."

Breast-feeding

When our kids were born, my wife decided to breast-feed them. Doctors agree that it's the best way to start a youngster out in life. And there is no more wholesome picture than that of a mother feeding an infant in this most natural fashion. But the cool part is how much bigger a woman's breasts get.

One night after our second child was born, I got to feeling a little romantic and started kissing my wife on the neck and rubbing her back. She was enjoying the attention, but she turned and said, "Look, Bill, this is all fine and good, but you can't touch my breasts."

I said, "What! You've got to be kidding!" Heck, that's like giving a kid a brand-new bike—with two flat tires. What good is that?

"I'm sorry, Honey, but they're sore," she explained, recognizing the hurt-child look on my face.

"Well," I countered, "How sore?"

She assured me they were far too sore for any sort of extracurricular activity. Needless to say, I read myself to sleep that night.

Well, a few days later, idiot that I am, I decided to have some fun and get back at her. She got to feeling a little romantic and started kissing my neck and rubbing my back.

After a couple of minutes, I turned and said, "Look, Baby, this is all fine and good, but you can't touch me down there because it's sore."

But instead of an argument, she just backed off and said, "Okay."

Meanwhile I started whining that it wasn't that sore. All right, I was begging by that time. And no, I'm not going to tell you how this particular story ended.

I was climbing onto the trampoline in our backyard and my neighbor asked, "Are you going to jump on the trampoline for a while?" I said, "Nope. I'm using the trampoline to put leaves back on the trees."

My daughter and some of her friends were enjoying a hopscotch game in front of our house. I was coming home and asked, "Are you girls playing hopscotch?" My daughter said, "No, we're just stepping on specific ants."

I was sitting in my living room with the CD player turned on. My friend walked in the house and asked, "Are you listening to a CD?" I said, "No, I have a really good band in the closet."

My wife and I were watching a drunk guy weave down the sidewalk. She asked, "Do you think that he's drunk?" I said, "No, he walks like that in case someone is trying to shoot him."

I was buying a ticket at the movie theater last week and the woman in the ticket booth asked, "Are you going to see a movie?" I said, "No, I want a ticket to watch the popcorn machine."

Last fall I bought a hot dog at a football game and a guy
in line behind me asked, "Is that a hot dog?" I said,
"Nope. It's a tubular Reuben sandwich."

We were at a pet adoption fair and a guy asked, "Are you going to
adopt a dog?" I said, "No, we're going to keep that brown one for a
week and then give it back just to mess with its mind."

I broke my wrist the other day and the bone was sticking out. I
rushed to the hospital emergency room and the doctor asked, "Did
you break your wrist?" I said, "No, I'm here for a prostate exam. I
use the bone for roasting marshmallows."

I was on a flight to Las Vegas and the man sitting next to me asked, "Are you going to do some gambling?" I said, "No, I'm going to count all the burned-out lightbulbs on the signs on the Strip."

My son and I went to a hockey game and he had on Wayne Gretzky's jersey. A guy in line at the concessions stand asked, "Hey, is Gretzky your favorite hockey player?" My son said, "No, I like Gretzky because he's the guy who drives the Zamboni machine."

I took my family to the circus and the lion tamer came out with the lions. My wife leaned over to me and asked, "Is that the lion tamer?" I said, "No, it's the lions' dinner. They like it to be alive before they eat it."

When *my* friend and I went hunting, we waited *most* of the morning and finally a buck came by. My friend asked, "Is that a buck?" I said, "*No, it's a doe wearing an antler hat.*"

My wife and I were driving down a street and stopped at a house that was for sale. The realtor happened to be there and asked, "Are you interested in this house?" I said, "No, we're interested in the For Sale sign. We collect them."

I was raking the front yard and my neighbor asked, "Are you raking leaves?" I said, "No, I'm combing the grass."

I was looking at an RV on the dealer's lot the other day and the salesman asked, "Are you planning a long trip?" I said, "No, I like these RVs because of their great gas mileage."

Last summer we were having a cookout and I was getting ready to chop some onions to put in hamburgers. My neighbor was visiting and asked, "Are you going to chop up that onion?" I said, "No, I'm going to hold this knife to its neck and demand its wallet."

I took the kids to the park with a kite and a ball of string. Someone asked, "Are you going to fly that kite?" I said, "No, I thought we would just drag it around in the dirt for a while."

We were in Hawaii and this woman walked by with one of those coconut bras on. My wife asked, "Do you think those are really coconuts?" I said, "No, she's just been out in the sun too long."

I bought my wife some roses for Valentine's Day. The guy selling them asked, "Are these for your wife?" I said, "No, they're for the gardener. He's done a really good job this year."

The last time I took my car to the car wash, the attendant asked, "Do you want us to wash your car?" I said, "No, just let it play in the sprinkler for a while."

My friend came back from vacation red as a beet and my wife asked if he had gotten sunburned. He said, "No, but I got a really good deal on body blush."

I was in a mall and heard a mother who was more than a little upset ask her child, "Do you want me to spank you?" The kid said, "No, I thought we would settle for a kick in the head."

My daughter came running into the house crying. My wife asked, "Did you hurt yourself?" She said, "No, I'm crying because I'm just so happy to see you."

I was encouraging my son to get ready for bed and asked if he was going to brush his teeth. He said, "No, I thought I would let them rot out so I can drink milk shakes."

Whales

Last year my wife and I went for our first whale-watching expedition off the coast of California. Let me tell you, it was really cool. We got to see quite a few whales and got very close to one in particular. As we watched, the whale made a high-pitched squealing noise.

Just then, everyone freaked out. They started jabbering excitedly, saying stuff like, "What'd he say? What'd he say?"

I hollered, "He just said, 'Wheeeeep!' That's what he said. Stop trying to figure stuff out!"

But I do think it would be really neat if someday we found out that whales could talk the same as you and me. Perhaps all these years they have just been messing with us with those little squeals and squeaks. Wouldn't it be great to catch a couple of whales talking underneath the water?

"Man, you should've been here yesterday," one would say to the other. "There was this scuba diver, and I went, 'Wheeeeee.' You won't believe this. *He started writing stuff down!* I laughed so hard I choked water in my blowhole!"

My friend and I went to the racetrack and saw a horse warming up by running around the track. "Is that a racehorse?" he asked me. I said, "No, it's a greyhound on steroids."

We went to Hawaii and a guy asked me, "Hey, is that girl wearing a grass skirt like I've seen in all the pictures of Hawaii?" I said, "No, someone put her dress through a shredder."

I was putting my bowling ball into the bag and my wife asked, "Are you going bowling?" I said, "Nope. I'm going to play extreme dodgeball."

I took my kids to the carnival and we were standing in line for the roller coaster. The ticket taker asked, "Are you going to ride the roller coaster?" I said, "No, we were going to run in front of it."

My son came in and said, "Hey, Dad, I want to play you a song on the piano. I'm going to play a song from *Harry Potter*." I said, "Oh, the movie?" He said, "No, from the book."

A lady came up to me and asked, "Are you wearing cologne?" I said, "No, ma'am, I just drank a bottle of Aramis and I'm sweating it out now."

We were eating dinner the other night at an Italian restaurant and I was having spaghetti and meatballs. Just as I was about to take a bite, the guy at the next table asked, "Hey, is that spaghetti?" I said, "No, it's extremely long rice."

I was putting luggage into the rooftop carrier on my car and my neighbor asked, "Are you going on a trip?" I said, "No, I like to take the suitcases to the park every once in a while for some fresh air."

My wife has a canary that sings all the time. One day our neighbor asked me, "Is that the bird doing all that singing?" I said, "No, the dog is a ventriloquist."

I was having breakfast at one of those all-night diners and a guy stumbled by and asked, "Hey, is that bacon and eggs?" I said, "No, it's a bowl of chili in disguise."

A man was plowing the snow out of a parking lot. A woman walked by and asked, "Where did all this snow come from?" He said, "We had it brought in so we could try out this new snowplow."

My family and I were watching a parade and someone behind us asked, "Is that the parade?" I said, "No, it's the line to use the Porta-Potties."

Snakes

Everyone I know seems to have at least one totally irrational fear—I mean one thing that just scares the living daylights out of them. For me, there's no question—it's snakes.

Before I got married, I had one date with this girl who had a snake for a pet. It was a 12-foot boa constrictor named Fluffy. We had been out drinking and the truth is we had way too much to drink. I'd had so much to drink that I had to keep looking at her belt to remember what her name was. Somehow or other, we ended up back at her mobile home. She lived in one of the tiniest single-wide trailer houses I'd ever seen.

She closed the door behind us and then did her best Marilyn Monroe impression. "I'm going to slip into something a little . . . more comfortable," she said with a quirky wink and what she must have thought passed for a seductive smile.

Heck, at that point, I'd had so much to drink I'd have thought Ernest Borgnine was sexy, so it didn't really matter. I just said, "Alrighty!"

After a few minutes, she came back from the bedroom/kitchen (and no, I'm not making that up. I told you it was a small trailer). This girl had on a sexy little negligee—and that snake wrapped around her neck.

Boy, that'll sober you up like a cold shower! In about two seconds, I was backing out the front door, sober as a judge, and thanking the good Lord that I was escaping with my life.

"No! Wait, Bill!" she pleaded as I clawed my way through the screen door. "Fluffy can wrap himself around us while we make love."

With one foot sticking out the door, I gave her my best Humphrey Bogart sneer and said, "No, he can't. 'Cause I'll kill him."

With that, I ran from there as fast as I could, afraid that if I looked back she would be swinging Fluffy around her head like a lasso.

I was wearing a bowling shirt and carrying a bag, and a guy asked, "Hey, are you in a bowling league?" I said, "No, I'm a really colorful doctor."

My family and I went camping and the forest ranger came up while I was stacking some sticks and logs and asked, "Are you going to build a campfire here?" I said, "Nope. I'm going to build a log home for a family of squirrels."

I was packing a suitcase the other day and my wife asked me if I was going on a trip. I said, "No, I just like to practice packing."

I was walking home from a softball game in my uniform and my neighbor asked, "Have you been playing softball today?" I said, "No, I'm just really early for a Halloween party."

I was standing over the stove boiling some water when my wife asked, "Is that boiling water?" I said, "No, it's really, really hot ice."

When my daughter was born, I handed a guy at work a cigar and he asked, "Did your wife just have a baby?" I said, "Nope. The cigar just had a litter and my wife won't let me keep them."

I was driving down a busy street and my muffler became detached from the car and hit the ground. I stopped to pick it up off the road and a guy on the sidewalk asked, "Did your muffler fall off?" I said, "No, I'm pretty sure it jumped."

We had a really big rainstorm and the basement filled with water. My neighbor and I went downstairs to look at the damage and he asked, "Did your basement flood?" I said, "No, we built an indoor wading pool."

I had the flu and was "tossing lunch" in the bathroom. My wife asked from the other side of the door, "Are you getting sick?" I said, "No, I just like the acoustics of this toilet bowl."

I was cutting down a tree with a chain saw and
my neighbor asked, "Is that a chain saw you're using?"
I said, "No, it's a really noisy hatchet."

I was eating a bagel in the coffee shop the other day and a guy
asked, "Is that a bagel?" I said, "No, it's a spare tire for my Yugo."

When I broke my arm, a guy asked me, "What is that on your
arm? A cast?" I said, "No, they just used more starch in my shirt."

I shanked my ball into the woods and was looking for it when another golfer asked, "Are you looking for a lost ball?" I said, "Nope. I'm looking for a place to hide one."

I had a For Sale sign in my car window and a guy in the parking lot at the store asked, "Are you selling the car?" I said, "No, I'm selling the sign, but the car goes with it."

I was setting out some weed poison when my neighbor asked, "Are you going to kill the weeds in your front yard?" I said, "No, I'm going to leave this out here and hope they commit herbicide."

One New Year's Eve I was buying 12 cases of beer for our neighborhood party. As I was walking out to the car, a couple in the parking lot asked, "Are you having a party?" I said, "No, I'm heading to an AA meeting and I'm in charge of refreshments."

Lions and Zebras

I've always wondered how animals know which of their prey is the weakest. You know, like when lions hunt zebras, they always go for the weak and the infirm. They always seem to know which one is the weakest zebra. Well, how do they know that?

I have a theory. Now it's nothing scientific, but I figure there has to be a squealer zebra—one little patsy zebra that doesn't want to get eaten and so he narcs on all his buddies.

He goes sneaking up to the lions' den. "Hey, fellas," he whispers. "Now here's the deal. There's a herd of us a couple of hundred yards down there. Now everybody's in pretty good shape—'cept Bob."

Then he looks around to make sure none of the other zebras are watching him. "Bob smokes. He'll be good for about 50 yards, then he'll start wheezing. That's when you guys can take him out."

Like I said, it's just a theory.

Some buddies and I were in a store buying supplies like tents, coolers, and such. The girl at the checkout counter asked, "Are you going camping?" I said, "No, the car broke down and we're going to rough it in the parking lot."

My sister came over to the house in her brand-new Jeep and my wife asked, "Are you driving that new Jeep?" She said, "Nope. I walked over and the Jeep followed me here."

The trashman forgot to pick up our garbage. So I called the sanitation department and the lady asked, "Is your trash outside?" I said, "Nope. I'm keeping it inside so it stays fresh until you get here."

I turned on the yard sprinklers and my neighbor asked, "Are you watering the yard?" I said, "No, I'm giving the worms a shower."

My wife was interviewing a lady for a baby-sitting job. The lady said, "I have to get home to check on my husband. He has had three heart attacks." My wife asked, "Did he live through all of them?" The lady said, "No, he died after the second one, but he's fine now."

I was driving to work on the freeway and another driver rear-ended my car. A cop pulled up and asked, "Did y'all have a wreck?" I said, "No, we were driving and the cars decided to mate."

My daughter walked into the house and yelled, *"Dad!"* I answered, "Yes." She asked, "Are you home?" I replied, "No, this is my personal voice-activated answering machine. Leave a message."

My son and I were going to the hardware store when
a fire truck went by. My son pointed at the truck and asked,
"Is that a fireman on that truck?" I said, "No, he's
auditioning for the *Village People*."

I was walking toward the bushes with a pair of clippers when my neighbor asked, "Hey, are you going to trim the hedge between our yards?" I said, "No, it's time for the squirrel's haircut."

I had just put up our Christmas tree when my buddy came over and asked, "Is that your Christmas tree?" I said, "No, it's the neighbor's. We're just baby-sitting it for the night."

I had a chicken on the kitchen counter and my son asked, "Are you gonna cook that chicken?" I said, "Nope. I'm going to dress it up and take it dancing."

I went to the drugstore and the girl at the counter asked, "Are you here to pick up a prescription?" I said, "No, I'm trick-or-treating for antibiotics."

I decided to paint *my* house and was putting everything out to get ready. My friend asked, "Are you going to paint the house?" I said, "No, I'm hoping that if I lay this all out here, the house will paint itself."

My wife was running her hand across my face because it was so smooth and asked me if I had just shaved. I said, "No, I sucked in really hard and pulled the hairs back into my face."

I took my paycheck to the drive-up window at the bank. When I handed it to the teller, she asked, "Do you want to cash this today?" I said, "No, I just wanted you to see how much I made this week."

I was clearing snow out of my driveway when a guy walked by and asked, "Are you shoveling the driveway?" I said, "Nope. I'm putting the snow back on the driveway. It was so much fun shoveling it the first time, I decided to do it again."

When I was in high school, I was stocking shelves in a store during the holiday season. A customer asked me, "Do you work here?" I said, "No, I stole this stuff last summer, but I'm returning it for the holidays."

My wife bought a vacuum cleaner the other day and it didn't work, so I took it back to the store. The saleslady asked, "Are you returning the vacuum cleaner?" I said, "No, I'm here to do your floors."

I took my son out of school one day so we could go deer hunting. When I told the principal what I was doing, she asked, "Oh, did he get a deer tag?" I said, "No, we're going to take our chances and poach one."

When I stopped at a light, my car quit running and there was smoke coming out of the engine. A guy walking across the street looked at me and asked, "Did your car break down?" I said, "Nope. We stopped so it could have a cigarette."

I was in the bathroom and my wife knocked on the door and asked, "Are you in there?" I said, "No, I'm in the kitchen and learning to throw my voice."

I was buying some dry cat food the other day and the girl at the checkout counter asked, "Do you have a cat?" I said, "Nope. I'm just refilling the candy dish at work."

I was taking care of my friend's house while he was gone. One night I was unlocking the front door when his neighbor asked, "Are you a friend of John's?" I said, "No, I'm a burglar. I called ahead and John left me the key."

The Carnival

I recently took my son on a carnival ride called the Scrambler. Its big deal is centrifugal force, which is not something I like to subject myself to. But I didn't want to disappoint my son, and so we got on the ride.

Once we were seated, I noticed it had a big bolt sticking out and the nut was just spinning around on the end of it. I thought, "That ain't right." So I tried to get the attendant's attention. That was when I got my first really good look at him. I noticed that his name tag proclaimed that his name was Earl, and I have to say, his outward appearance did not instill a great deal of confidence in me.

Trying to get Earl's attention was about as simple as getting a shot of tequila at an AA dance. Much to my chagrin, the ride started without warning.

Falling victim to the enormous centrifugal force, I quickly found myself smashing my son into the corner of the seat. While trying to pull myself off of him so he could breathe, I continued yelling at Earl, "Slow down! Slow this darned thing down!"

However, my pleas must have sounded to Earl like, "Let's see just how fast this puppy will go!" I'm now convinced that ride operators must get paid a bonus every time someone pukes on their ride.

After the ride had ended and the security guards had peeled me off Earl, I casually walked over to the trash can and lost everything I had eaten for the last six months. It really pained me to give Earl the satisfaction—and the cash bonus—but I didn't have any choice.

As we walked away, I heard Earl hollering joyously, "He blew in cart four! That's another hundred bucks!"

A guy had a sweatshirt with a star on the front and somebody asked, "Are you a Cowboys fan?" He said, "Nope. I'm a fan of Galileo's."

I was in a hotel one time and the television remote didn't work. So I walked down to the front desk and told the receptionist. She asked, "Are you still in the room?" I said, "No, I'm in the restaurant. This is my clone talking to you."

My wife was curling her hair with a curling iron. It slipped and burned her eyelid. We rushed to the doctor's office and he asked, "Was this an accident?" She said, "No, ever since I was a little girl, I've been dying to heat up a curling iron and stick it in my eye."

My car quit running the other day—the gas gauge was on "Empty." When I walked into the gas station with *my* gas can, the attendant asked, *"Run out of gas?"* I said, *"No, I got too much and I'm returning the rest."*

The kids and I had just finished coloring some eggs for Easter when my friend came over to the house, took a look at what we were doing, and asked, "Are those Easter eggs?" I said, "No, they're psychedelic hand grenades."

We were having a yard sale when a guy walked up and asked, "Are you having a yard sale?" I said, "Nope. We're keeping the yard and selling the house."

I was going to a funeral the other day and had a suit on. My friend saw me and asked, "Where are you going?" I said, "To Joe's funeral." He replied, "Did he die?" I said, "No, we're having a dress rehearsal so we'll be ready when he does."

My wife bought some holiday nutcracker soldiers at a store the other day. When she was checking out, the clerk said, "Oh, I just love nutcrackers. They are so cute. Did you get those here?" My wife replied, "No, they just like running errands with me."

My wife was in the kitchen unpacking groceries. I asked her, "Did you just get back from the store?" She said, "No, the refrigerator exploded and the food just happened to land in these bags."

It was pouring rain when I went to take my driver's test. When I walked into the DMV the lady asked, "Is it raining?" I said, "No, I'm nervous about the test and have already started sweating."

I needed to replace a door in our house. When I took the old door to the store, the clerk asked, "Do you need a new door?" I said, "Nope. I need a new house and just want to see if the door will fit."

I went to visit *my* father and took *my* dog along. When we parked in the driveway *my* dad asked, "Did that dog ride all the way with *you?*" I said, "No, he drove part of the way."

We had some new neighbors move in next door. As we were standing there talking to them the man asked, "Is that your house?" "Nope," I said. "It's the dog's and we are just his pets."

I walked up to a fast-food restaurant counter and told the girl I wanted to place an order. She asked, "Now?" I said, "No, tomorrow. But I wanted you to recognize me when I did."

I bought some doughnuts for the family, but by the time my son got out of bed, there was only one left. He asked, "Is that the last one?" I said, "No, the others are hiding, waiting for you to find them."

I put a Ping-Pong table out on the street with a sign that said "Free." A guy drove up and asked, "Is that table free?" I said, "The sign is free, but the Ping-Pong table is 20 bucks."

Butter Statues

On a recent concert tour we stopped at the Iowa State Fair, which is one awesome fair—one of the largest state fairs in the country.

One of the more memorable novelties I recall was a six-foot statue of Garth Brooks, carved out of butter. It was amazing, yet somehow very strange. It made me wonder about the lady who carved it. When did she realize she had that ability to carve butter? It probably started at the dinner table.

"Hey, Mom! That's a dang fine dog you carved out of the butter bar."

"Well, thank you, Jimmy."

"You know, you ought to go on to something bigger. That Garth Brooks is a nice-lookin' fella."

My question is, "*Why?*" Why would you carve a six-foot statue of Garth Brooks out of butter? The only thing I could think of was that the lady had way too much time on her hands.

And the shame of it is, as wonderful as that statue was, all they were going to do was melt it down. Who'd ever believe her? She would be at a party somewhere, bragging to her friends, "I carved a six-foot statue of Garth Brooks out of butter."

"Bull—!"

"I sure did."

"Well, where is it?"

"Oh, they melted it down and poured it on that popcorn statue of Alan Jackson."

My son was on the soccer field when a mother of one of the kids came up to me and asked, "Are you watching your boy play soccer?" I said, "Nope. I'm here to use a Porta-Potty. Our bathroom is broken."

The other day I was leaving the house and stopped to take my car keys off the key rack by the front door. My wife asked, "Are you going somewhere?" I looked at her and said, "Nope. I thought I would throw the keys in the field across the street and see how long it takes to find them."

I was sitting at a bar enjoying a beer when the guy next to me asked, "Hey, is that your beer?" I said, "No, it's my urine sample. I just want to keep it close."

When I was going to Chicago I had left my cell phone at home, so I stopped to use a pay phone in the airport concourse. My friend, who was traveling with me, asked, "Do you need to make a call?" I said, "No, my left ear is cold and I'm going to use the phone to warm it up."

We went to the pet store to buy a litter box for our cat. The clerk asked, "Did you get a new kitty?" I said, "No, I got a dog but he thinks he's a cat."

I went to the bursar's office to pay my daughter's college tuition. The cashier asked, "Do you know her name?" I said, "Nope. She hasn't been born yet. I just wanted to get a jump on it."

I had just been to the barber and my friend asked, "Did you get your hair cut?" I said, "Nope. I had my head enlarged."

My son is in the high school marching band and it was going to play at halftime. A guy asked my son, "Are you in the band?" He said, "No, I'm a football player. We just got new uniforms."

A woman was sitting under a hair dryer at a beauty salon
and another woman asked, "Are you drying your hair?"
The first woman said, "No, I'm pretending to be Buck Rogers
in the 25th century."

I was at the post office and the woman in front of me in line asked, "How much is a 37-cent stamp?" The clerk said, "It's 50 cents: 37 cents for the stamp and 13 for the stupid question."

I was sitting in the car in the driveway getting ready to go to work, when my son asked, "Are you leaving?" I said, "Nope. I'm gonna sit here and see how long it takes to run out of gas."

I was trying to put up a tent in 30-mile-an-hour winds. The park ranger came up and asked, "Having trouble putting up your tent?" I said, "No, I'm just practicing my parasailing."

The Secret of a Happy Marriage

I'm convinced that one of the reasons my wife and I have stayed together so long is that we don't play board games together. We learned not to do that early on.

We once tried playing Pictionary—the game where you have to draw clues on a piece of paper so that your partner can guess the word. By the time the game was over, we had lawyers on the phone. We were with some friends and as I recall, the men were winning, but just by a tiny bit. The ladies needed only one word to win the game and my wife was the guesser. I swear, it happened just this way. Her partner drew a *straight line*—a straight line! My wife immediately yelled, "Hydroponic farm!" Incredibly, it was the right answer!

The women were shrieking, "Yes! We win! Yes! Yes!" while the guys were looking around like a UFO had just landed in the living room. Then one of the guys finally said aloud what we were all thinking: "How'd she get that?"

"Meet Mrs. Milton Bradley," I said sarcastically.

That was the last time we ever played a board game together. In the ensuing argument, after everyone left for home, we weren't just considering divorce—we were actually talking custody arrangements. It just isn't worth it.

We went to the drive-thru in a fast-food restaurant and all the lights were off. The girl looked through the window at us and my wife asked, "Did the power go off?" The girl said, "No, we work in the dark. It's more of a challenge that way."

I was working on my son's Volkswagen with the engine in the back. My wife walked into the garage and said, "Oh, is the engine in the rear?" I said, "No, it's in the front. This is just the spare engine."

I sprained my knee the other day. When I limped into the doctor's office, he asked, "Did you hurt your knee?" I said, "No, I'm working on a new dance step."

I put my groceries on the supermarket checkout counter and put the plastic divider down. After scanning my items, the checkout girl tried to scan the divider and finally asked, "Do you know how much these are?" I said, "They're free with any purchase."

My grandfather recently picked up his new hearing aid. When he was walking out of the audiologist's office, a woman said, "Oh, you got a hearing aid. Are you having trouble hearing?" He said, "Nope. I just wanted surround sound all the time."

I was taking my clothes to the Laundromat when my neighbor asked, "You going to do laundry?" I said, "No, I just joined a nudist colony and I'm throwing these clothes away."

When I was in grade school, my sister's ferret died. When I got home, she said that she had buried it. My mother asked, "Oh, did it die?" My sister said, "No, I just wanted to see how long it would take for it to dig out."

I bought the kids a trampoline the other day. As I was unloading it my neighbor asked, "Are you going to put that in the backyard?" I said, "Nope. I'm going to put it in the hallway so the kids can literally jump into bed."

I was working in a shoe store and a man called and said that he had bought a pair of black shoes. He asked, "What color polish should I use?" I said, "Use white—it will turn black in the sun."

When I was backing my truck down the boat ramp at the lake, I drove too far and it got stuck in the mud at the end of the ramp. I called a tow truck and when the driver arrived he asked, "Were you backing into the water?" I said, "No, I started from the other end of the lake and made it this far and got stuck."

I was getting rid of an old couch, so I set it out on the sidewalk for the garbage men. A couple of hours later, the doorbell rang and a guy asked, "Are you throwing that couch away?" I said, "No, I like to be comfortable while waiting for the mail delivery."

Clipping Coupons

When my wife and I were first married, like many young couples we were on a very tight budget. Being thrifty, my wife became a coupon clipper. In those days, I loved her all the more for it, but now I will pay *whatever* the groceries cost. Just please, oh please, don't make me use coupons!

On Sunday afternoon, you don't mess with my wife. She sits in the middle of the living room and those scissors just fly! With scraps of paper floating around the room like confetti, she screams stuff like, "Creamed corn, 50 cents off! Artichoke hearts at two for a dollar! I don't believe this."

But the worst part is when we get to the grocery store. We fill a cart with enough groceries to feed the Partridge family, and then, in the checkout line, she whips out this encyclopedia-sized book of coupons. And wouldn't you know there's always a guy in line behind us moaning, "I just want to get these grapes. They're going to be raisins by the time this chick is done!"

I was laying tile in a new house. I turned around and two police officers were standing there. They asked, "What are you doing here?" I said, "I'm a burglar and when people aren't home I break in and retile their floors."

We were at church one Sunday when my wife was eight months pregnant. A woman came up to her and asked, "Are you going to have a baby?" My wife said, "I don't think so. We're hoping for a miniature pony."

My friend from England came to visit me in Texas. While we were in a store the clerk said, "You don't sound like you're from around here." My friend said, "No, I'm from England." The clerk replied, "Wow! Did you drive all the way here?" My friend said, "I tried, but the bloomin' car sank."

I was in the hospital and a friend who was there visiting his brother saw me. My friend asked, "Are you sick?" I said, "I'm not. I just enjoy wearing this really cool backless gown they give you."

I was going inline skating the other day and had my skates in my hand and a guy asked me, "You going Rollerblading?" I said, "Nope. I got a flat tire and thought I would strap these to the wheel of the car and give it a shot."

My son was selling raffle tickets in our neighborhood and a lady asked, "Do I win a prize if they pick my number?" My son said, "No, you just get the thrill of hearing your name called."

I went to the store the other day. When I got to the door I pulled on it and it was locked. So I started walking back to my car and another guy asked, "Are they closed?" I said, "No, I just wasn't strong enough to open the door."

I got pulled over by a policeman and he asked, "Can I see your license?" I spaced and said, "My driver's license?" He said, "No, your fishing license. It's such a nice day, I thought you and me would go fishing."

A buddy of mine jumped into the swimming pool. When he came up he was hitting himself on the side of the head. I asked, "Got water in your ear?" He said, "No, one of my eyes is stuck."

I came out of Starbucks the other day with a cup of coffee. A man stopped me and asked, "Are they open?" I said, "No, I just broke in and made a cup for myself."

I was sorting through some fishing lures at the store the other day and a guy asked, "Are you looking for fishing lures?" I said, "Nope. I'm looking for matching earrings for my wife."

After fishing with a buddy, we pulled our boat into the dock and lifted out this big string of fish. A guy on the dock asked, "Y'all catch all them fish?" I said, "Nope. We talked them into giving up."

I told my boss that I was going outside to smoke. He asked, "A cigarette?" I said, "No, a ham. I have cut back to two hams a day."

I just put a new satellite dish on my house and my neighbor came over and asked, "Are you getting satellite television?" "No," I said. "The rest of my family lives on Mars."

One day I ran out of gas. As I was walking to the gas station with a gas can in my hand, a guy stopped and asked, "Did you run out of gas?" I said, "No, I thought I would walk the rest of the way and give the car a rest."

I was standing in a hotel lobby in front of the elevators. A guy walked up and asked, "Are these elevators the ones that go up?" I said, "No, these go side to side. The up ones are down the hall." He walked away!

My wife and I were going out to dinner and she asked, "Is *that* what you're wearing?" I said, "Nope. I'm just wearing this out to the car. I'm gonna change in the restaurant parking lot."

The battery in my car died. When the tow truck came my car was hoisted onto the back of the truck. My neighbor saw what was going on and asked, "Getting your car towed?" I said, "No, we're mating them and hoping to get a Mini Cooper."

About the Author

Bill Engvall has been doing stand-up comedy for more than 20 years. His popularity has soared since he joined Jeff Foxworthy, Ron White, and Larry the Cable Guy in *Blue Collar Comedy Tour*, which has had two movie releases and spawned *Blue Collar TV* on WB.